making whole

rachel h

Making Whole.

Copyright © 2022 Rachel H

All rights reserved.

Other than brief excerpts for reviews and commentaries, no part of this book may be reproduced by any means without permission of the publisher.

ISBN: 978-0-6453272-0-5

eBook ISBN: 978-0-6453272-1-2

Cover Designer – Matthew Huckel

Editor – Susan G Scott

Scriptures taken from the Holy Bible, New International Version®, NIV®. Copyright © 1973, 1978, 1984, 2011 by Biblica, Inc.™ Used by permission of Zondervan. All rights reserved worldwide. www.zondervan.com The "NIV" and "New International Version" are trademarks registered in the United States Patent and Trademark Office by Biblica, Inc.™

This book is published independently under the imprint ALittlePoetic Publishing.

For enquiries, visit rachelhuckel.com or email rachelhuckel@gmail.com

making whole

contents

the goodness of stillness   9

the mystery behind purpose   49

the promise of restoration   91

afterword   137

a prayer for the poetry book

may it become less about the one
who made it and more about the reader.
and may in time, it become less about the reader
and more about the One who made them.

the goodness of stillness

useless

i spent my summer making myself useful.

taking a class.
getting my driver's licence.
buying shares.

and by march,
it all crashed.
the market, not the car
(thankfully).

i wanted to laugh.
we spend our time
making ourselves useful
by doing useless things.

in autumn, i took a train to the ocean.
let my hair down.

i thought about nothing except
how beautiful the waves were.

oh, those were a few useless hours.
(i think they made God's heart sing.)

t-intersection

yesterday i was driving and i came up to a t-intersection. i needed to turn right but i sat there for ages because the traffic was so heavy in both directions. i almost cried. i thought, *the world is going too fast and there is no space for me.*

maybe i'm just overtired.

i haven't been sleeping that well either. i keep having dreams that i am playing piano in a symphony and the conductor is waving frantically at me to keep up but i don't know the piece well enough. i haven't been rehearsing.

lately, it all feels like a performance.

truthfully, i am foraging for permission to drop out of a race that i never wanted to be in. but all people hand me are phrases like, 'you're doing fine'. sometimes i crawl into bed exhausted and wonder if dropping out is the more courageous thing.

but i'm doing fine.

(am i the only one who feels like it's all a waste of time?)

a series of semi-related thoughts

there is a drought in my country at the moment.

a) lately i've been thinking about how much i take for granted and how if the rain were to come, the city would sigh and raise umbrellas while our farmers would raise their hands in relief.

b) lately i've been thinking about what i really need. and if hope is enough to get it. you see, i keep praying for rain without taking an umbrella. (i think my faith is running dry.)

c) lately i've been wondering about all the things a man might be down on his knees asking for, and if another man is out there hoping for the opposite.

d) lately i've been thinking about how strange it is to be human—always yearning for a change in the weather, always wanting greener grass.

a series of semi-related thoughts pt. 2

a) at a certain point, the familiar no longer feels comfortable. the familiar is an ache in your bones.

b) i don't know why i thought change would make me tired. i am exhausted from routine. from having the same conversations in the same places.

c) time feels like a tyrant rather than a playful friend. is that my fault? did i push it away?

d) i don't think we were designed to draw each day the same way.

e) i don't think we were built with creative minds to make living something we can do with our eyes closed.

tiny and tremendous

with all the time spent here, we start noticing things in our homes. the dust along the skirting boards. the cardboard boxes in the tops of our wardrobes. they are labelled 'winter coats' and 'old dancing costumes' but that is not all we find. we find lost languages that we were once fluent in but have long since forgotten. we take the time to revisit them. relearn them. and the tenderness of it all leaves a familiar taste on our tongues. remember when we once had wild dreams? when we gave ourselves the time to try them on like enormous winter coats and dancing shoes that our toes couldn't reach the tips of? oh, we have long since outgrown them. we have forgotten how to speak the language of our youth. but we take the time, and it comes back to us, slowly. we shake the dust off our dreams. we dance around the house. the clock ticks over and the hours soften. we, like time, are turning tender. a tiny and tremendous transformation.

the kookaburra

we fidget with the threads
of the couch cushions.
gaze longingly out our
living room windows.
we watch the eucalyptus leaves
shake in the autumn wind.
(what we wouldn't give to be
moved by the breeze.)

then through the ruffled leaves
we see him—a small brown bird,
all feathered and free.

the kookaburra laughs at us
because we don't know
how to be still.
we don't know how to take
only what we need
and to return the next day
as faithful as ever
in the generosity of the earth.

i watch him sit on his perch,
a smug little creature
who either knows something
we don't or is
just happy in his not knowing
and in this way
he has found peace.

either way, i am glad
that someone is laughing.

i am glad that someone thinks
the barriers
should not contain our joy.

wildly welcome

i've sat here for quite some time now
just listening
and feeling my way around
the silence.
i want to find a word for the rain.
the tender way it falls
onto a broken world.
the clogged storm drains
and the frizzy hair of strangers.
the upturned lips of umbrellas
and the hands that scramble
for control.

but it will always be
a reckless visitor
or, in this case,
a wildly welcome house guest.
and all i can do
is watch and wait.
listen to it whistle a song
that i will never find the words to.

birthplace

silence is the
birthplace of song.

the isolation of beauty

i was driving home at five pm.
the daylight hadn't quite been swallowed
but the sky was open-mouthed
and yawning.
not quite yet
asleep.

the jacaranda trees
were stretching their spindly arms.
almost dancing
in the final light of dusk.
they blurred together as i passed them,
congregated on the hill
along the exit of the motorway.

i was speeding away from the day—
the things i didn't quite say right,
the tasks that were left to be done tomorrow—
when the moon came into view.

he seemed to be stuck.
pasted in the centre of the purple-painted sky.
so full and bright
that i had to slow down.
i had to still my anxieties
just to make room for his presence.

he did not wait for permission.
did not have the patience
to be told it was night
before he appeared.

at the roundabout at the top of the hill,
i gave way to a blue calais
who flew past me.

where is anybody going
when the sky has given way?

i watched the flurry of cars
with their anxious pace,
wondering why we bond over busyness
but stand in isolation when we are still.

must beauty always give way to busy?

i took one last look at the moon
before i turned and drove off.

he looked a little lonely.

pinball

i wonder what the world
looks like from space.

i imagine it looks like
seven billion balls
bouncing frantically
around

as though stuck inside
a pinball machine
in a busy games arcade.

a metaphor for modern life

i don't know the names of my neighbours
but i can tell you their grass is greener.

wonder

every morning
i carve out space to
drink coffee and
tackle the most pressing
task of the day.

usually, an essay
or an important email—
something worth dedicating
my best work to.

only this morning,
i decided
to carve out a space
to do nothing more than wonder.

i wondered
how heavy a breadcrumb
is to an ant.

i wondered
if i could make a painting
using only
the colour of coffee.

i wondered
what the world would look like
upside down—
if we would walk on the sky
and look up to the grass.

it was some of *my best work*.
even though i had
nothing to show for it.

tomorrow, i might allow myself
to wonder again.

i might let myself wonder
how different things would be
if we stopped putting
all our other work
before the task of
being human.

cloud traffic

this afternoon,
i was trying to get some work done
when i made the beautiful mistake
of looking at the clouds
outside my window.

i couldn't pull my head
out of them.

i watched how they moved—
slowly colliding,
passing through one another
at a peaceful pace.

i thought about how life
feels like entering a highway
as a learner driver—

you must match
the signposted limit
because if you go too slow,
everyone will pass you by.

yet here were the clouds,
content with the traffic
they were creating,

knowing that slow
doesn't mean stuck

and happy for the world
to blur beneath them.

oh, they didn't teach me
anything about life.

they just existed.

(sometimes that's enough.)

dose of dreams

i stir clouds into my coffee,
each morning
swallowing my daily dose
of dreams.

rising

the trick is to watch the sky.
the day breaks open lazily.
it wriggles its toes into the light.
bats its eyelids.
once.
twice.
then stretches its heavy moonlit arms.
lets the night roll off its shoulders.
slowly.
then comes the dawn of a new era.
it is called today.
you see, rising has never been a routine.
it has always been a victory.

slow dance

i am not sure if time is going too fast or i am going too slow. the world is always ticking. june. july. august. amber light. red light. green light. there are rhythms but i am falling behind their metronome. i think i am meant to be moving but i watch it all blur like houses from the train window. it has always been safer inside. or has it? the rain does not touch me but i still feel it. drops slide down the windowpane and without warning, slide down my cheeks too. my mother often jokes that my mind works separately from my legs and my fingers; i often joke that her mind works in to-do lists. but we are both quite serious. she would like to be better at living and i would like to be better at loving.

i want to be less noun and more verb but i spend so much time sitting still with the names of the people i love floating around in my head and trying to show them feels like another unrealised dream. though not all dreams need a destination. sometimes they just need to be nurtured in the quiet of a journey. is it enough? and when you try to take deep breaths and your lungs still only feel half full, is it living? my mother and i wrestle with how to shift our weight between head, heart, and hands. it is an odd balancing act, but we keep living and keep loving, not because we are good at them but because we have met grace.

we have so much to learn from each other. we have always said this. we just haven't listened until now. she teaches me that love is the reason you move. even when you think you can't. even when legs and fingers and mind are in a bitter argument, they will always reach an agreement when it comes to labours of love. and in turn, i teach her that to love life, you must slow dance with it to rhythms of amber lights and rain down windows. because if you're always moving, how are you ever going to give yourself a chance to be moved by the chaotic beauty of it all?

my relationship with time

days pass me by like strangers on the street and i don't stop to notice them. i think this is where it all started. this sonder. this desperate yearning.

time and i aren't enemies. not exactly. but i think i would prefer that. time and i are the equivalent of talking to fifty people about nothing more than the weather. in other words, i want to get to know it better.

after all, i have lived here for two decades now and have only just noticed how nightfall looks like earth slowly closing its eyelids. or that even shrivelled up daisies open their buds in the spring. and that somehow the sum of these small truths carries more weight than anything else i've held today.

it is hard to quantify what a well-lived day is. let alone a lifetime. but i think it is because i am measuring it all wrong. i am breaking in new days like the same old pair of jeans. i am wearing time skin-tight and wondering why it is wearing me down.

in the grand scheme of things i am only a blink to the sky, only a neighbour to the daisies. and yet i yearn for life to know me as more than someone who rushed past it. someone who didn't slow down for long enough to notice it for what it is:

a work of art. a mystery. a miracle.

riches

why do we ever look further than the promises of God? when did we decide there must be a pot of gold at the end of His rainbows?

for we are looking for riches, but the colours hung in the sky already sing out the riches of His love and grace.

look up—He's always been more than enough.

spring clean song

there are piles on my bedroom floor
of all the clothes i own.
there are some i don't remember buying
and others i have outgrown.

i need to clear some wardrobe space
just to get some peace of mind.
and to come up with a system
to make things easier to find.

it's a little overwhelming
but i take it piece by piece.
and after a while, those big piles,
slowly they decrease.

as i work i hum praises
to my Father up above.
it feels like a chance to start anew,
a reminder of His love.

it's true what they say:
how less makes you free,
how you'll find you have something to wear
once you clear out the debris.

i love this soft worship,
it reminds me of the soul:
how the less that's on your mind,
the more you can see the goal.

so, Lord, give us strength
to put it all back in place,
because the only outfit we truly need
is one in which to run the race.

"However, I consider my life worth nothing to me; my only aim is to finish the race and complete the task the Lord Jesus has given me—the task of testifying to the good news of God's grace."

– Acts 20:24

the wideness of grace

my heart was beating at an unnatural pace
when I stepped out into the street.

it had been a busy day,
the unfinished tallies of the day's work
threatening to spill over into the next.

I was aware of the deadlines,
of the twelve unanswered texts on my phone,
all asking something
or, rather,
asking something of me.

I began to walk.
past neighbours' mailboxes.
past the house with mosaics in the window—
rainbows made of torn crepe paper pieces.

the sky was dimming,
weaving itself into a deeper blue
when the thought came to me—
how unlike the sky we are,
not big enough to cover everything.

I walked with that thought for some time.
I lifted my heart to pray.

how that blanket of blue comforted me,
revealing the wideness of grace.

as I returned home, I felt it cover me.
I felt more peace than I have in weeks.

knowing
i don't have to be all things.
knowing
a God who already is.

poetry by the speed limit sign

people also have limits
to how fast
they can go.

sabbath

one day a week, take yourself out of this world
you have built around you.
a world of deadlines and missed phone calls.
a world of emails and overdue fees.

and place yourself back into the world that
was built not on human anxieties,
but on the breath of the Father.

sit for a while on the floor of the forest
or the grass on the hill by your house.

wait and learn the truths
that are new to your heart
yet older than the grass itself.

feel the rhythms which
all of creation is dancing to.

note the orange tips of the leaves
like fire edging its way closer to the roots.

marvel at how colour is acutely aware
of what season it should arrive in—
an understudy that waits patiently
before flying onto the stage.

remember that you, too, were created
to live inside these rhythms.
the ebb and flow of the ocean.
the push and pull of the breeze.
what have they been trying to tell you?

stay a little longer.
feel the grass bending beneath your weight,
the leaves crunching under your skin,
and ponder your design.

even the bees were not created
to hum with constant energy.

rest a while.
consider the goodness of stillness.

consider this rhythm part of
an age-old worship song.

gift

it took me years to realise that
the sabbath is not a burden;
it is a gift.

stillness

i have always loved stillness. i have always thought that the world is the loudest when the streets are quiet. i think this is why i write—because there is something to be said about the way the trees reflect the afternoon light, and how even facing east you can see the sunset by watching shadows flicker over rooftops. but i still haven't figured out how to say it. i keep trying but sooner or later, i have to admit that this world is too miraculous to describe with a heart that is only human and an alphabet that is only twenty-six letters. i think this is why God finds me in the stillness (why i hear Him most clearly through whispers). it is because most of the time, i am guilty of missing His miracles. but at the end of the day when i slow down, stop trying, and start being still, i can only write the same truth: *God, out of all the metaphors i hold in the palm of my hand, not one of them lives up to You.*

forget what you
were told about
the best
morning routines.

the first thing you do
in the morning
does not have to put you
on the path of success
but on the path of
faithfulness.

leave the morning workout
aside for a minute.

resolve to write
your to-do list later.

for now, just sit in the
soft mercy of sunrise
and greet your Creator.

watch how He
resurrects the light.

know that all things
are in the process of
being made new.

and whilst you were sleeping—

even you.

just be with me

each morning for months
i rose and came before
the throne of God,
asking what He required of me
that day.

without fail,
each morning i'd hear
the voice of God
whisper back,
'just be with me'.

i am still trying
to wrap my head around
a God who only wants
my heart,

a God who doesn't
need me to work for Him

but *lets* me participate
in the goodness of
His kingdom.

a God who wants
me to pursue *Him*,
before anything done
in His name.

i am still learning to meet God
as a friend,
not a commander,

still learning to explore
the depths of His heart—

*how wide, how long,
how high, and how deep*
it is.

when was the last time
you carved out a quiet space
to just sit with the Lord?

and did you feel just as
profoundly loved and
miraculously lost?

empty spaces

i have learnt that there is a quiet strength in the times that require us to rest or to wait. we are trained to believe that these are spaces we should only enter when life demands it: when we are wrestling with illness or burnout, when we are hoping for an answer we can't control like a job offer or a positive pregnancy test.

but i believe there is beauty to be found in the empty spaces, even though they are often hollowed by a vague yet persistent sense of grief. it is only in these empty spaces that we truly come to terms with our humanity. we are forced to confront our limitations— the brokenness of our bodies and the loss of our control.

it is only in these times that we understand that our role in God's kingdom is only a small part of the story. we may think that nothing is happening because we ourselves are not working when, in reality, God is working behind the scenes for our good. He is growing our character, multiplying the work we have already done and preparing new paths for us.

the important thing to remember is that God works in mysterious ways. it is His plan for His kingdom purposes. so, we can rest and wait, knowing that the time is far from wasted. knowing that God is making something beautiful out of the empty spaces.

grace

but grace doesn't always look
like a chance to start afresh.

sometimes grace is having the patience
to let things grow
amongst all the uncertainty,
amongst all the mess.

02

the mystery behind purpose

this place

you've placed me here with purpose,
not left me without hope.
sometimes i fear you've forgotten me
but then you let down a rope.

you pull me out of sadness.
send me back on my way.
i don't know where i'm going,
but i know i'll thank you someday.

perspective

some days i want to get out of my body.
see things through a different lens—
one that hasn't been tainted
by twenty years of living.

the idea haunts me.

there are so many lives i haven't lived.
so many people who haven't lived mine.
(would they do it any better?)

and i know we read to learn.
travel to grow.
to find ourselves in places
that aren't our own skin
(get some perspective,
or whatever they call it these days).

i am not old by any means.
just curious.
my bones aren't aching
unless you count longing as an ache.

oh, some days i am just a little restless.
that's all.
just overwhelmed with possibility.

i consider myself lucky.
i consider that free.

beautiful places

i admit, sometimes i think more about how to get to beautiful places than how to make the place where i am beautiful.

i loved this world

i want to look back on my life
and look back on a world map
and not pinpoint the places i've been
but rather say,
'i loved this world
with everything that was in my hands',
even if i never got to travel it at all.

art travels

(even when we cannot).

the writer's world

you may not understand
why i stop to watch the leaves fall,
for there's another world
and it beckons me with its call.

for years it has been knocking,
calling only certain souls.
it's the whisper through the trees
and the quiet breeze that rolls.

it's searching our humanity
for the wild and restless brains,
for those who see greater beauty
but also see greater pain.

i am yet to meet anyone
who knows this world so well
but the journeys of the leaves
have a lot of stories to tell.

they spread hope from the people
who entered this world to roam,
but they liked it so much
that they now call it their home.

thoughts from when i first fell in love with art

maybe other people see something different in the world too. maybe they just don't stop for long enough to write about it. or maybe they don't know what to make of it. or maybe they just don't care. i think that's what art is: picking up a pen or a paintbrush or an instrument and trying to make people care.

what is poetry to you?

is it just something read at funerals and weddings? is it reserved only for these occasions when we dress up in black and white or is it something in between? to me, poetry is colour. it is for any time. anywhere. poetry is the sky, the ocean. but it is also the linen tablecloth at a family dinner. it is the debris afterwards. the imperfections. like a condiment stain in the corner of the tablecloth. that ends up landing it in the bargain section of a second-hand store. *poetry is a lost property box for moments.* that's where the words begin. by uncovering what is left behind or forgotten. it is a place to put the memories others abandon. *poetry is a museum for feelings we want to revisit.* a home for the thoughts that don't belong elsewhere. that we can't quite say out loud. it is the freedom of an open space. and the honesty of close quarters. something we feel as a brush past our knuckles. like strangers on a sardine-can train service. *poetry is a carrier service for connection.* a postcard sent or unsent. where we address what is missing. sometimes it doesn't matter what we say. it matters who we are saying it to. even if it is only the page. *poetry is an escape from living in our own minds.* a chance for captive thoughts to break free. what is poetry to you? this is just the beginning of what poetry is to me.

a confession

i don't like art museums. or the poetry they teach in schools. i have never been to an orchestra but i don't think i'd enjoy the stiffness. of trying to make myself be moved when i think i'm meant to.

this is not to say that there is something wrong with cordoning off your art. or becoming so good at the violin that you can play in front of suited strangers.

but i love the kind of art that turns up in unexpected places. the kid i hear practising piano while on a walk around my neighbourhood. the doodle on the back of a take away menu that is stuck up on the fridge. the conversations that accidentally end up sounding poetic.

which is an outrage to some—those who want art to be curated. who think that it's only for the chosen few.

i confess: the other day i felt my heart shift looking at what was only a few paint strokes on the page.

i heard myself become the usual critic, saying, 'but anyone could have made that'.

to which my heart replied, 'exactly'.

exactly.

the poem will not stand without the heart

the heart nearly always
has a hand in the matter.

you cannot will yourself to write
using just your mind,
using just the tools they give you in school:
metaphors, stanzas, rhymes…

i don't care what they say
about constructing a poem.

you cannot build a poem
on the foundation of
the paper assembly instructions they hand out.

the poem will not stand

unless you churn the matter over
until you feel yourself soften.
then pour your heart out
like concrete over the ground.

you cannot base a poem
on tone, rhythm, craft…
they cannot hold up a house
for the reader to dwell inside.

a poem will never be a safe place for anyone,
never be revisited in the late hours of the night
until you cement your troubled self
in the words with which you start.

the first thing you should know
about structure is that

the poem will not stand without the heart.

recently i have been pulling poetry
out of all kinds of strange places.
i think it is some act of defiance.
i think the more battered i become,
the more i crawl under my skin,
desperate to find something
the world cannot break.
oh, it can't all ache.
it can't all ache.

it can't all ache.

what poets know about painting

i keep trying to turn my heart off
because i'm afraid i can't be used
when i'm always painting over
a heart that's too easily bruised.

a poet becomes a painter
when they don't want to feel the way they do.
i, too, would swallow yellow paint
if i thought it could get rid of the blue.

the artist & the scientist

i see God in art.
which is a foreign concept
to my friend with the science brain.

he says that he sees God
in patterns.
in the reliability of his movements
over time.

but i find God in stories,
drawing closer to Him
as i grapple with beauty.

i will never understand
facts and data
the way i understand
metaphors and symbols.

but perhaps i do not need to.

perhaps we have a God
who is either intimate enough
to speak the language
of both our hearts

or perplexing enough
to reveal His presence in
a million indecipherable ways.

i'm starting to believe in
both

a God who finds us
and a God who is waiting
to be found.

listen to enough stories
and you will realise
that they are all the same.

in every story—something broken.
in every story—an act of grace.

is this not a pattern?
is this not a science that
proves itself true over time?

you can look at it as evidence
or look at it as art.
either way,
we reach the same conclusion:

God is present in the midst
of our brokenness.

i say, *how beautiful.*
he says, *how constant.*

we are learning each other's languages.

but i suspect
we will never wrap our heads around
all the languages of grace.

all art is, in some way or another, telling a story. and i have found that no matter what story i am telling, there is always a deeper one behind it.

when you write over a long period of time, you look back and see the growth that was occurring. the transformation in yourself, in your relationships, in your community...

it's humbling to realise that God has been the real storyteller this whole time. you can see His grace and faithfulness over a season of your life.

but even within a single piece of art, you can see evidence of His grace. because what do we have to bring to the table? a pen and a piece of paper and a mess of feelings. but God takes whatever we bring and shapes it into something beautiful through us.

that's why i believe that all art is telling a bigger story.

all art is pointing to grace.

make art

not because it prepares you
for *what* you are going to be
but because it prepares you
for *who* you are going to be.

i do not yet know
what i'm going to spend
my days *doing*.

but i know
who i'm going to spend
my days *being*.

i make art
because no matter where i end up,
i want to be creative.
i want to be thoughtful.
i want to be kind.

how i want to live

i just want to write by the water
and earn a fickle income
and love and love and love.

where He's taking me

i have given up
trying to steer the ship
in a certain direction.

the wind always carries
the sails across
to the wrong side of the water.

it picks up and takes me
with it and really,
there's nothing i can do.

the wind must know
something i don't—
must believe there's something
i should be headed for
across the mysterious
swell of the sea.

so i let the day carry me
off course once more.

i work, yes,
but really
i'm just waiting.

just waking up to
watch the wind

and wonder
where He's taking me.

storyteller

not knowing the direction of your story doesn't make the words you are writing a poorly-thought-out plan.

it means you are trusting that the empty spaces will be filled by the One who tells better stories than any of us can.

sandcastle kingdoms

when my parents used to take
my sisters and me to the beach
during the school holidays,
they would always pack
a bucket and spade.

we'd run down to the water's edge,
limbs all chubby and flailing,
and find the perfect spot
to spend the day—

just close enough to the water
that the sand was still wet,
but with enough distance
that the waves wouldn't reach us.

with our stubborn determination,
we would begin to build
sandcastle kingdoms.

my older sister would shovel
clumps of sand,
i would pack it down tightly
with my palms,
and my little sister would
scavenge for shells to decorate
the walls of our towers.

if we were lucky,
she'd find a twig for
the top of the castle—
a leafy flag to sway in the wind.

once we had finished,
we would stand guard
over our sandcastles,
so that no one could ruin
the kingdom we had created.

yet throughout the day,
the tide would pull in.
and a wave would inevitably
collapse all our efforts
in a single go.

that's when we'd run back
to our parents—
cry in our father's arms.

he'd scoop us up lovingly
and carry our exhausted
bodies back home.

how easy it is to laugh at
our naivety now.
of course the castles
were not built to last.

but somehow, i am still
making my own kingdoms
out of sand—

still protecting
things that cannot withstand
the waves.

over and over again,
i end up retiring
my exhausted body to
the loving arms of my Father
as He reminds me

i was never made
to build kingdoms;
i was made to live inside His.

**God has always been up to
something i cannot see.**

God has always been up to
something i cannot see.

God has always been up
to something i cannot see.

master artist

they say we are all born artists—
that our lives are what we paint.
some rush to fill it with colour,
and others keep their outlines faint.

some work their whole lives
hoping to create something grand,
so even late at night
the paintbrush never leaves their hand.

others only hope
that their colours will not die.
they are busy making memories
before the paint runs dry.

me, i've only ever wanted
to fill the canvas well—
for it to be a story
that i am proud to tell.

but lately i just can't seem
to get the outline right.
the story that i want to tell,
i just can't seem to write.

i've felt so disappointed
and struggled to understand
how if we are all artists
it is so out of our hands.

so one day i took my heart out,
drove to the edge of the sea.
i took all my bottled-up questions
and finally set them free.

i asked why all my carefully
laid-out plans and lists
keep slipping through my grasp
like sand between my fists.

while i was waiting by the water
for an answer that never came,
i watched the ocean move like a masterpiece
spilling out of its frame.

imagine there was an artist
who created the sky and sea.
drew it all together so each drop
is where it is meant to be.

imagine that same artist
holds my life in His hands
and is painting it with purpose,
not following my plans.

i walked beside the water
as i let that truth sink in.
we are all born artists
but the master artist is Him.

my story is written perfectly
for it is not my own.
i stayed just a little longer
before i made my way home.

how could i ever think
that any of the plans i had in mind
could be better than a future
that He has purposefully designed?

blessings

like water from the skies,
everything runs its course.

like raindrops, heaven rolls out
blessings that turn into
blessings that turn into
blessings.

even when i don't realise.

all that falls will one day rise.

a feeling i can't shake

i don't know where i am going but i think i am getting closer.

good gardener

our God is a good gardener,
even when it hurts to grow.
every day He works in our lives
in ways we will never know.

He gets up early in the morning
to tend to the budding shoots
and water the fertile ground
that is slowly bearing roots.

His timing is held carefully
in His soil-stained hands.
He knows when to sow the seeds
and when to reap the land.

but sometimes we can doubt
if our God is really good
because He gardens us in ways
that we don't think He should.

when He prunes our dormant branches
or pulls weeds from the ground,
we worry that this rooting out
will last the whole year round.

but the gardener is patient,
returning each morning with care.
because He knows the kind of fruit
His plants will one day bear.

just know a time will come
when our gardens will come alive,
and everything that was cut back
will soon begin to thrive.

our God is a good gardener,
even when it hurts to grow.
every day He works in our lives
in ways we will never know.

an unshakeable thing

my faith may not be
an unshakeable thing.

it is as restless as rivers.
as fickle as dandelions in the wind.

my faith may always be moving
from doubt to confidence,
from hope to despair.

it may change with the seasons—
withering through winter
and strengthening in spring.

my faith may take on
new forms day after day.
i cannot trust it to remain
as it is.

but maybe i do not want it to.

maybe my faith
was never meant to be
an unshakeable thing,
but was made to rest in the mercy
of someone who is.

stargazer

you've always taken the night shift on dreaming,
always loved watching the world fall asleep.
and it is at this time that the galaxies
hand down secrets for you to keep.

it is why you know the reason
God made the distant stars so bright—
so even when the page turns over to darkness
we remember the author of light.

so when the heavy curtain of night falls,
you know it is not the end by any means,
because you've studied the sky long enough
to know He's still writing behind the scenes.

there is still a congregation of stars singing
and against them, how does your voice compare?
but oh, stargazer, you keep singing anyway
because part of you belongs up there.

river

purpose is not a straight path;
it is a winding river
that widens the closer it gets to the sea.

mysteries

creation hides its mysteries
beneath the forest floor.
it keeps the keys to old secrets
washed up along the shore.

and if you listen closely
you'll hear the truth it holds:
your purpose is a story
that is slow to unfold.

take the forest for example,
with its carpet of leaves
that once hung like curtains
draping proudly from the trees.

their purpose isn't over
because they rot underground
to become food for the same tree
on which they could once be found.

and as the shells were once part
of the ocean's smallest treasures,
they now make up more sand
than we could ever measure.

and upon hearing this secret,
we must choose not to forget:
our purposes are stories
that are not finished yet.

the ants

nothing is too small
to have purpose.

consider the ants.

and how easily
they get inside
the walls we have built up
because they are
the only things
tiny enough
to break through.

landscape

you belong here.

and are capable of shaping
the world around you.

if you are ever in doubt,
consider the way
the rain can move mountains
over time
because it is so
relentlessly insistent
of its place.

reckless

this whole time i have been thinking,
i want to move,
but not knowing where to,
and in waiting for that answer to arrive,
i have missed the whole point of departure.

yes, i have been restless
because i have not been reckless.
have not leapt and
trusted God with the landing.

have not allowed my heart to go before my head.
have not placed courage before understanding.

03

the promise
of restoration

battle

each morning i wake up and must be quick—to run outside and sit with the Lord before i listen to what the world has to say.

faith always feels like a battle in this way.

why i read the bible first

each morning
when i check my phone
i think,
'when will there be
good news?'

but is this not
what the gospel means?

lessons from earth

the mist over the mountains
taught me that there is
beauty in the unknown,
and that you should keep walking
even when you don't know
where you're headed.

the birds flapping their wings
on their first flight
taught me to have courage,
even if you're afraid of falling.

the setting and rising of the sun
taught me that it is okay to rest,
as long as you get back up
to try again.

the wildflowers taught me
to grow with perseverance
and bloom with grace.

this earth taught me
kindness,
forgiveness, and
strength.

but this world only taught me
how to destroy it.

a second-hand poem

today i wrote a second-hand poem.
which is to say,
it has all been said before.

i read the newspaper
and see the same news.
a different body. a different headline.
but the same heartache.
it has all been said before.

i know there is kindness in the world.
people pick it up
but keep forgetting it
in all the wrong places.

on the train this morning,
i watched someone hand back
loose change that had fallen out of
the pockets of a stranger.
but he did not want it.
he left it behind on his way to work.

how i longed to pick it up,
to pass on the remnants
of that stranger's kindness.

but all i did was write about it
in a second-hand poem.
it has all been said before.

oh, if it has all been said before,
what will it take for something to be done?

big things

i don't know how to write about the big things.

don't know how to whittle poverty down into a poem. it would be like trying to pull down the night sky by a loose thread and weave it into a handkerchief.

some things are too big to fit into the pockets of our jackets. some things we can't carry around with us.

here's something i do carry around: the memory of an old man waiting for the same bus as me. he was sitting on the bench, his meagre groceries in a shopping buggy next to him.

i watched as he tore open a packet of reduced finger buns and ate them as though each one was a gift.

i don't have an ending to this story.

i wish i did.

but i can't whittle poverty down into a poem.

do you hear me?

i don't know how to write about the big things.
i don't know how to write.
i don't know how.
i don't know.

hands

it all hurts so much
that i don't know what to do
with my hands

except close them tightly
over each other

and pray.

uncomfortable

we need more poets who don't flee to the shores of the sea or nestle in the corners of upscale coffee shops. we need poets who will journey to the hopeless places. who can sit in the discomfort of a bus shelter. who will write about the cans and cigarette butts littered on the ground. who will let their hearts break over the words a father speaks to his young son. who won't turn away when their eyes meet the sunken gaze of a hurting child. poets who know that they have a place off the page. who won't hesitate to use their hands as much as they use their hearts. poets who can admit that they can't make everything beautiful, no matter how good they are at writing, because there are some kinds of brokenness we don't have the vocabulary for yet. we need more poets who are unafraid. who believe in something so wholeheartedly that when they write about the hopeless places, their work still hums with hope. and listen, i am not saying that is the kind of poet i am. but i hope, one day, it will be.

the other side of the story

in the dull lecture theatre,
students cram in at 8:30 in the morning.
our coffees are carefully balanced
on makeshift desktops
and there is just enough
space left to fit a small laptop.

we are all still
half asleep. even the lecturer
is similarly dishevelled.

people often ask me
what you learn in
international studies
and i give an answer
that will satisfy small talk.

what i should say is:

the way i thought the world worked
was nothing more than
a story i'd been given to swallow.
this is what i am learning.

there is a girl in the front row,
in line with the air conditioning.
her hoodie strings are
pulled tightly.
each week she chooses
the same spot and each week
she shivers.

and this morning,
i shiver too—
at yet another cold,
uncomfortable truth.

i emerge from the
lecture theatre at 9:30
and head to my elective
writing class.

it is an odd mix:
politics and poetry.

people often ask me
why i chose a degree in
international studies
instead of creative writing
and i give them an answer
that will satisfy small talk.

what i should say is:

i don't know exactly.

it just seems to me
that if i am going to
tell stories about the world,
i should at least learn
about the other side of them.

unless we are first moved

i write about the little things because that is what moves me. you can tell me about the scale of the problem but it's always going to come down to the leaf litter on the ground, the crunch underneath my steps, and my face floating in and out of the autumn shade. you can tell me about deforestation and i can sit in lecture theatres with a straight face but it isn't until i go outside and feel these tiny movements that my heart understands. poetry is a small thing in the face of this big world but we cannot move unless we are first moved.

tiny churches

once, i was shown a video of space.
as the lens zoomed out, the earth became
this tiny dot on the screen—
a freckle on the face of the universe.

everyone in the room fell silent in awe.
i thought, *am i meant to feel something?*
is there something wrong with me that i don't feel
immediately aware of my Creator?

perhaps that's the thing about revelation—
sometimes it comes in a grand epiphany,
and sometimes it comes by following
a bread crumb trail.

i find myself aware of my Creator
by following traces of tiny things like

the curiosity in a child's eye.
the wake patterns left by ducks in the water.
the weeds poking through train tracks.

i call them small interruptions.
i call them tiny churches.

a nudge to worship.
a trail leading home.

the economy of trees

i wrote that title
in the notes of my phone
on the way
to my boyfriend's house
after university.

but that was a long time ago.
i've graduated university
and that boyfriend
is my husband
and i've compiled
178 more notes
on my phone

of titles and phrases
for poems that
i will never come back to.

yet, something about
this title keeps
resurrecting it from
the graveyard of
my phone notes
to the forefront
of my mind.

it is not unusual
for the poet to beg
the poem into existence

but it is quite unusual
for the opposite to occur—

for the poem to grab
the poet by the pant leg,
begging to be written

but here we are.

so, what is there
for me to tell you?

i can tell you about
that day i was
leaving university.

i went there for
my political economy class.
we were going over
the market crash of '08:
who caused it and
who paid the price.

(funny how little overlap
there is in such
equations.)

when i enrolled in university,
i said i'd never study
politics or economics,
only poverty.

until i realised
how deeply
the latter is rooted
in the former.

i still have
so much to learn
about the way the world works,
but sometimes
i wonder if i really
want to.

knowledge is power
but power only
seems to become
someone else's poverty.

on the bus ride
home from class,
i read a book
about trees.

it said that
when one tree in the
forest is dying,
the other trees
sacrifice their nutrients
to care for it.

they transport them
to the sick tree
using the underground
root system

even though they may never
yield a return
on their investment.

i thought about
how much we have to learn
from the economy of trees.

oh, that was a long time ago.

(but if i'm being honest,
i've been thinking about it
ever since.)

the anatomy of the earth

i wish they taught us about
the anatomy of the earth:

how it is always half asleep.
how it is made up of 71 percent water
and 7.8 billion hearts
and if you listen closely,
how it keeps singing

despite.

souvenir

i spent the day at the mountains.

walked along the thin trails
and admired the movement of
the shadows over the valley—
the treetops which swallowed
each passing shred of sun.

breathing in green,

        breathing out green,

until late afternoon.

then in the car ride on the way home,
as nature's architecture was interrupted
by tall buildings,

i ran into a small sadness
that i hadn't taken a single souvenir
from my travels.

not even a leaf from the ground
or a photo of the cloud-covered sky.

oh, what does that say about
the nature of my heart?

that i spent the car ride home
pondering what i took from the day

and never once what i gave.

imagine

imagine a world in which we travel
to give more than take.

ocean between our dinner tables

as a young teenager, i was handed a nightmare
that left me sweating in my sheets.

i was sitting at my family's wooden dining table,
eating the dinner that was in front of me.

across from me was a girl my age
whose plate was empty.

but i continued to eat.
and eat.
and eat.

i wanted to shake the version of me
i saw in that dream.

i fought with my bed sheets,
screaming in my subconscious that

it wasn't like me.
i would share my plate with her—
i would never turn my back on someone
across from me when what they needed was
the very thing i had in my hands to give.

something shook me awake then.
and i heard it say,

no, you wouldn't.

so why do you turn your back on people just because there is an ocean between your dinner tables?

philosophy

it was coming up to closing time
at the bookstore where i work.
i was slicing through sticky tape
with paper scissors,
packing down the cardboard boxes
from the day's deliveries.

there was only one man in the store,
browsing the second-hand section—
books of withered pages and cracked spines.

when he came up to the counter,
i absent-mindedly asked him,
would you like a bag for these?
he had chosen a stack of books
by Peter Singer and Rachel Carson.

no, don't worry, the man said,
*my generation destroyed the environment,
it's our responsibility to fix it.*

i smiled.
i am not unacquainted with the philosophy.
i have spent three years
in university classrooms
discussing who made the mess
and who should be responsible for fixing it.

i think poetry is pointing out the mess,
philosophy is pointing fingers, and
politics is pointing at absolutely anything else.

there is nothing i can contribute
that has not already been
said.
argued.
whittled down.
picked apart to within an inch of its life.

but i will say this:
when i was seven, my parents gathered
my sisters and me in a room.
there was mud on the carpet, and they said,
*if no one is going to own up to it, you are going to
have to clean it up together.*
even though i know they noticed
the footprints were the size of my shoes.

perhaps responsibility has since swollen in size—
with names like the polluter pays principle,
or poetry, philosophy, politics.
but the sentiment is the same.

last semester, in the middle of
a heated argument over who was responsible
for reducing carbon emissions,
a student stood up,
can't we all stop arguing and just do something?

the class laughed.

i thought,
*this is someone who is
going to change the world.*

puzzle

when i was in primary school,
my dad attempted
to complete a 1500-piece puzzle
on the dinner table.

it was a picture of an eagle
against a clear blue sky,
which meant it was nearly impossible
to tell half the pieces apart.

he worked on it for weeks.

we all wondered when we were going
to have space to eat at the table.

when he came close to finishing,
i took a piece of sky
and hid it from my dad
so that he would come
an inch within finishing,
but never quite get there.

it was a cruel joke, yes,
but it wouldn't be the last time
i'd pretend a piece of the puzzle
doesn't exist.

sometimes i look at the world
and become the piece of the puzzle
that i hide.

because it is a terrifying
and time-consuming process
to find where i fit in.

what can i do
when there are billions
of other pieces and
it's so much easier
not to try?

but then i think of the eagle,
with his wings spread wide

and that oddly shaped
hole in the sky.

blame

if there is good and evil,
on that equation—where do we lie?
when we wouldn't hurt a neighbour
but because of us, they die?

when water rises over a nation's shores
we look for someone to blame.
but pointing fingers was only ever
a great time-wasting game.

when children sort through piles of waste,
whose old phones do they find?
not mine, we say, because it's easy
to turn eyes that are blind.

when a discarded bottle ring
becomes a turtle's noose
we are quick to hold someone accountable
but even quicker to cut ourselves loose.

we didn't nail Jesus to the cross
but just because we were not there
doesn't mean our sin did not add weight
to the cross He had to bear.

so are we good or evil?
or are things not so black and white?
have we turned people just like us
into enemies we have to fight?

i know you want a reason
for why the world is such a mess.
and the brokenness of humanity
seems too hard to address.

i know you don't want to hurt anyone
or live with any kind of sin,
and it's hard to think we can't escape it
because of the world we're living in.

where do we turn to make things right
when all we see is wrong?
we look up to the One who planned
to redeem us all along.

so for now we wait and try to make
things a little better while we can—
knowing we can be both fallen people
and part of God's redemption plan.

the heart of God

i keep praying that
my heart will love
more like God's,
then am surprised
when it aches.

meant to be

once my sister climbed a ladder
where she thought she wouldn't be seen,
took a brush to the leaves in our backyard
and painted the brown ones green.

and maybe this meant nothing
but i still watched her paint that tree.
if only it were that easy
to put the world back how it's meant to be.

some kinds of sadness

there are some kinds of sadness we can't wrap our heads around. we can only wrap our arms around those who feel it.

flight

the water may weigh down a feathered wing,
but what the rain dampens will dry.
now you are heavy but soon you will sing.

when birds see the clouds' grey colouring,
they flock to branches up high.
the water may weigh down a feathered wing.

i know you to be a delicate thing,
laden with the need to cry.
now you are heavy but soon you will sing.

the birds have nothing but a song to bring,
while they wait, yearning to fly.
the water may weigh down a feathered wing.

your heartache will give way to worshipping,
one day you'll understand why.
now you are heavy but soon you will sing.

the rain will lift and, on the upswing,
you will turn your face to the sky.
the water may weigh down a feathered wing.
now you are heavy but soon you will sing.

some things that don't make sense

a) how a bookstore is one of the best places to be but the shelves are lined with lost forests.

b) how the city lights look like a fairytale from afar but they are a tragedy of the commons.

c) how a hymn at a funeral is a heavenly sound but it is sung from mortal mouths.

d) how humans are such beautifully destructive creatures—part wreckage; part redemption.

where faith is found

perhaps faith is not found
in the answers
but in the questions.

the woman who asks why

wisdom doesn't come from
the woman who knows it all;
it comes from the woman
who admits how little she knows.

i choose to learn from her.

because the more i live,
the more i realise that
theology textbooks
only take us so far.

there are some questions
to which there are
no fitting answers.

like *why does a good God
allow so much suffering?*

i know the usual explanations.

i know that there is sin
and that broken people
have a habit of
breaking others too.

i know that God is capable
of intervening but allows
some situations to
play themselves out,
even when it hurts Him too.

i know that all suffering
in this life is temporary
and that tears will soon
be wiped away.

i know.

but knowing
isn't enough, is it?

if that were the case,
i would be unfazed
at the sight of a dead child,
or a single mother
living on the streets.

because *i know*
why the war broke out.
i even *know* what caused
the stock market to crash.

i *know*,
but i still don't *understand*.

and i don't want to learn
from anyone
who says that they do.

i don't want to take after
any woman
who doesn't weep before
the throne of God

and ask Him why.

shameless audacity

in one of my last weeks
at my parents' house,
i went on a prayer walk
early in the morning.

i prayed for the usual things
my wayward heart
is prone to crave:
direction.
certainty.
grandeur.

then when i entered
the cul-de-sac
which shortcuts
back to the house,
i realised i'd
forgotten to pray
for anyone but myself.

so i prayed for
those i love:
the man i was about to wed.
the friends i held dear.
the family i lived with.

when i returned,
my mother asked,
'what did you pray about?'
and not wanting to admit
my half-hearted attempt
at thinking of others,

i said in jest,
'i prayed for you
the whole time.'

but she didn't laugh.

she said,
'well, i expect to see
some answers then.'

i've been mulling this over
for weeks now.

this shameless audacity.

this faith in the
power of prayer
that i had not realised
was lacking in
my own heart.

i had been praying
simply because
i thought it was
the right thing to do.

(as though i was the
only thing that prayer
could make better.)

(as though God
didn't know my
every intention already.)

yet here was a woman
who was expectant
to see change
because of prayer.

this afternoon,
i will go on
a prayer walk again.

only this time,
i will ask for
big, bold things.

i will pray with a heart
that is expectant
for answers,

because of
the shameless audacity
my mother taught me.

~~how to~~ pray

i pray in the bathtub.
i pray when writing poems.
i pray the beginning of prayers,

        unfinished prayers

(church may be the only time i utter an amen).

i pray erratically,

            sporadically,

i fall asleep in the middle of prayers.

i pray aloud
sometimes
      by myself
sometimes
      in front of others.

and i stutter through
all of them.

i leave long silences in prayers

and in other prayers, i can't keep up with
all the things i want to say.

i pray for this person

                and that person

and i pray for myself
a lot too.

i don't think i've ever fully finished
praying about something before

        i pray about something new.

yes, i am not very good at
praying

        but i still think
        my prayers
        will do.

i need to pray for bigger things

i think i am praying to a god
who doesn't exist.

by this i mean,
i am praying to a god
who does only logical things,
proportionate things,
things within the realm
of human capability.

i admit, my prayers
have become pocket-sized,
even though our God
can carry the whole world
in His back pocket.

i need to pray for miracles
like a farmer prays for rainfall—
each day looking upwards
to ask for transformation
in this land.

i need to ask for restoration
in unfathomable amounts.
something like a generation
turning to Jesus.
something like a war-torn country
knowing peace.
something like plains of destruction
being made new.

there is an audacity
to these prayers,
yes,

but wouldn't it be even more audacious
to pray asking God
to move a blade of grass
when He has told us
He has the power
to move mountains?

creation writes its own prayers.

the sunken eyes of twilight close.
the waves bow down against the shore.
the mouth of the desert is dry
and yearning
for a taste of renewal.

what do i have to add to that?

except amen.

amen.

making whole

a little girl sits at the foot of her Father,
a map of the world in her hands.
and it hurts in places she's never felt before,
hurts with a desperation she can't understand.

she runs her fingers over the borders,
completely lost for what to say.
and seeing the girl with no place to put her grief,
the Father prompts her to pray.

so she hands the map to her Father
and hopes the hurt will start to heal,
knowing the grief that is in her heart
is only a glimpse of what her Father must feel.

the little girl sits at the foot of her Father,
telling Him all that she can't control—
just a fragment of a broken story
He is busy making whole.

Afterword

I can't tell you how grateful I am that you picked up this book.

The idea for this poetry collection began with its namesake poem, 'Making Whole'. I used to have a map of the world stuck next to my reading chair. Over the course of months, I spent countless hours staring at it, trying to comprehend the pain that the world was in.

When I would sit down to read the Bible or pray, I felt overwhelmed with the dissonance between being a woman of faith and living in a broken world.

They must, I thought, have some connection.

I thank God for His grace in helping me pen the poem, 'Making Whole'. It was the first reminder (of many) that God has a plan for our world and a purpose for each one of us.

It was these two concepts that I began to dwell on in the following months. I wondered how my life and worldview would transform if I kept in mind that God is the author of both.

There's a Bible passage I want to share with you:

"So from now on we regard no one from a worldly point of view. Though we once regarded Christ in this way, we do so no longer. Therefore, if anyone is in Christ, the new creation has come: The old has gone, the new is here! All this is from God, who reconciled us to himself through Christ and gave us the ministry of reconciliation: that God was reconciling the world to himself in Christ, not counting people's sins against them. And he has committed to us the message of reconciliation. We are therefore Christ's ambassadors, as though God were making his appeal through us. We implore you on Christ's behalf: Be reconciled to God."

— 2 Corinthians 5:16-20

I love this gospel truth that God is reconciling all things to Himself. I cling to the hope that, one day, He will restore everything that is broken. Our earth and its people; you and me.

I wonder how different the world would be if we leaned into God's plan and pressed closer to the purpose He has given us: *ambassadors of reconciliation.*

Of course, I am still young and don't pretend to have any answers. You would have noticed that I only have questions.

I hope this book gives you permission to wrestle with them.

I hope you will join me in considering the goodness of stillness, the mystery behind purpose, and the promise of restoration.

All my love,

Rachel

About the Author

Rachel H is a poet and poetry editor based in Sydney, Australia.

She is usually found with a coffee in one hand and a pen in the other.

Her first poetry collection, *Fleeting Things*, was published in 2020. *Making Whole* is her second book.

rachelhuckel.com | @rachelhuckel

www.ingramcontent.com/pod-product-compliance
Lightning Source LLC
Chambersburg PA
CBHW020325010526
44107CB00054B/1981